Praise for *Grief, Guts and Grace*

"What a truly lovely book. I thought at first it was the perfect book for the specific moment of bereavement. However, as I began reading, I found Theriot-Broussard had much to teach me, and that any time is the perfect time to reassess grief. As anticipated, her grief brought back my own over loved ones I have lost. Yet quickly I did not mind, for my heart and thoughts opened to her perspective; that grief means growth, yet only if we work with it. She conveys that idea so much more sensitively than I have here. I never thought of grief as work before, but view in that manner, one realizes God sends it to the soul for a purpose.

As a writing teacher, I could see how very valuable the suggestions of journaling are. As one who believes in God, I appreciated her conversations with Him. The most charming and deeply touching aspect of this book was the author's description of daily life without that wonderful man whom she called Pookie. The bill with this name scrawled on it, the ending tube of toothpaste, the matter of the house to be attended to and the lawn mower all told me a lot about the woman writing the book, and how she arrived at growth and understanding through grief. I feel gratitude for having read this book; it is very valuable!"

—Judge, Writer's Digest
21st Annual Book Awards

"Joan, you have put into words, quite effectively, the sentiments of one who has endured the pain of losing their beloved. Your unfailing devotion and dedication to Bradley, as well as your steadfast faith resonates profoundly. It is inspirational."

—Kelly T. Cahill, MD, Family Medicine

"Joan Theriot-Broussard writes about the death of her husband at 51 years of age, and her process of grieving. She makes the point well that grieving is a process. We will all deal with the death of someone close at some point in our lives, through varying circumstances. Still, it is an experience like no other - so final and so life-altering to those who remain. And yet it may not be as final as one thinks. How we handle this grieving process is what will determine how we heal from it. Ms. Broussard touches on many things that one may not think of having to deal with and offers her advice. It is also important, to her healing and also to the reader, that she has hope of seeing her husband again after she joins him in heaven.

I chose this book in response to the recent death of my father. I had not dealt with a close family death in some time, and was interested in the assistance of someone else's experience. What I found was permission to grieve in my own way, with helpful advice on how much and what to do. This book will help others dealing with this issue, including my mother. It can help while one is in preparation for a loved one's death, since much can be accomplished in the months leading up to it to minimize regrets. It has made me think differently about those remaining in my life and how to maximize good memories and quality of the life that remains."

—Mary DeKok Blowers, *Readers' Favorite*

"I gave your book to my cousin. she loved it. She said you included a few items that she felt other books or articles did not include. Things that helped her to normalize her feelings. One was the freedom you may feel after the loss. She loved her husband but always had to hurry home and now she doesn't. That is a new freedom even though she would prefer to have him. Reading your book helps."

—Sylvia Marcantel, RN
Hospice and Palliative Care Consultant

Grief
Guts and Grace

SECOND EDITION

JOAN THERIOT-BROUSSARD

Grief
Guts and Grace

If you have the guts to work through your grief,
God will give you the grace to survive it and find your joy again.

Grief, Guts and Grace
Initial Copyright © 2013 by Outskirts Press. All rights reserved.
Second Edition Copyright 2015 by Tate Publishing.
Re-published 2018 by Joan Theriot-Broussard. All rights reserved.
Printed & Distributed 2018 by IngramSpark

Scripture quotations are from the New American Bible, copyright 1970 by the Confraternity of Christian Doctrine, Washington DC, including the Revised New Testament, copyright 1986.

No part of this publication may be reproduced, stored in a retrieval system or transmitted in any way by any means, electronic, mechanical, photocopy, recording or otherwise without the prior permission of the author except as provided by USA copyright law.

Cover design by Junriel Boquecosa
Interior design by Honeylette Pino

Published by Joan Theriot-Broussard
107 Beacon Drive, Youngsville, LA 70592
Printed and Distributed by IngramSpark

Published in the United States of America

ISBN: 978-0-578-41396-9

Self-Help / Death, Grief, Bereavement

Religion / Christian Life / Death, Grief, Bereavement

For John Bradley Broussard, "Pookie"
my husband, my lover, and my friend of nearly 30 years.
I learned many things during our life together:
to live simply, love deeply, and keep promises.
You asked me to tell your story;
here's to keeping my promise.

And to my husband, Carl Thanas Broussard,
who has been so generous
as I write about my life before him.

Acknowledgements

There are many people who helped to shape this author into being. Lyn Holly Doucet was my first Spiritual Director and was truly my first midwife. She helped me to find the guts to allow this woman/writer to be born. Her insight about how much I wanted to "do the work" helped me to actually get down to it. I remember telling her, "When I grow up I want to be just like you." Actually I have grown up to be just like I am supposed to be—me.

Father Don Piraro was the Director of the St. Charles Retreat Center where I received my certificate of completion as a Spiritual Director. Father Don is the first person with whom I trusted my soul, who did not allow me to put him on a pedestal, and would tell me the truth even when I wanted to stop chasing after it. Thank you, Father Don, for your wisdom and your gruffness as well as your tenderness. You taught me that those negative voices in my head were not people from my past, but my own voice keeping me from allowing God to touch my soul. Your lessons enabled me to recognize that voice and let God minister to my wounds.

I devote much love to my son Macy and daughter-in-law Monica, my daughter Sarah and her husband Ronnie. Their combined love and support have always been the stars that light my pathway into the future when I didn't think I could begin to rebuild a new life of my own. Their presence in my life makes it worth living. My first grandchild, Bryce Paul, was my shining beacon in the midst of the darkest moments of grief. It was this child, born six weeks before Bradley's death, who gave me a glimmer of hope to go beyond my grief. It was in him I first saw what my life could look like; and to my granddaughters, Brooke and Bailey, in whom I see glimpses of my own inner child.

My heartfelt thanks go to two women who never tired of hearing my stories of sadness, at all hours of the day and night: my sister Gale Bonin and my coworker Virginia Gail Evans. These two women have been my spiritual guides and mentors. Without them I could have never entered into "the work," much less attempted to finish it.

I share a unique gift of laughter with my older sisters, Irmaline Loyce and Gale. I love to make them laugh and cherish our childlike bantering when something quite ordinary tickles our funny bones. Whenever this happens, it is inevitable that one of us will wet our pants in laughter. My three brothers, Larry, Ronnie, and Ames Theriot, have contributed unwittingly to my feeling of belonging for many years. Their love and concern for my happiness, regardless of how long the lapse between our visits, have kept us connected to our roots.

My parents, Woodrow and Luda Theriot, provided the example of what it takes to meet life's challenges. The character and work ethic they instilled in all of their children made for strong and resilient citizens. Daddy was my first role model for being a widow. The lessons he taught me in the short time we shared this role before his death still hold true for me today.

Thanks to the extended family I received when Bradley and I married: Marie Louise and Antoine Broussard, Mary Ann and Loifey Maturin. They accepted this insecure, skinny young girl into their lives. They showed me what it is to love and share their hearts. They have my respect and sincere gratitude for all the kindness and generosity they showed me in the years I have lived among them.

There are countless others who have been my inspiration, mentors, and sources of strength and unconditional love and friendship. I want to express my gratitude to those who fit this category in grand style: Beth LeBlanc, Charles Harkless, Ernest Gradney, Faye Douet-Sonnier, Pam Bourgeois-Buillard, and Bruce and Wendy Cardon.

Thanks to Sally Trahan and Sue Credeur, the first to share their grief work with me. We helped each other for the first year of bereavement counseling to see the light and catch a glimpse of our life to come. Thanks also to those who have attended the Journal through Grief series that I facilitated at Hospice of Acadiana in Lafayette, Louisiana. Sharing our grief work in a safe environment enables us to give hope one to another, which says that you can do this "work" and survive.

One of the most precious rewards of doing my work of grieving is finding my joy and the ability to love again. God has blessed me with a precious man with whom to share my life. Carl is my partner, both spiritually and emotionally. His love has opened my heart to new heights, and his generosity has no bounds. What a gift God has given me with this man! I love you.

Salve for the Soul

In the act of being still, there is a knowing;
knowing that God is real and is truly there.
I am scared, Lord; make me brave.
I have faith in your divine love; give me courage.
Sorrow does not occur in order to break our human dignity,
but to open the heart so God can act.
Hope lies in braving the chaos
and waiting calmly with trust in the God who loves us.
Lord, I will tear the heart of my soul in two,
and you must lie therein,
like a salve that heals and renews my spirit.

Contents

Foreword 19
Introduction 21

Chapter 1 My Grief 27
           Journaling My Grief 29
           The funeral Is Over, Now What? 34
           Personal Belongings 36
           Legal Matters 36
           Was It a Message from Him? You Decide 38
           Little Things Aren't So Little 40
           Home Maintenance 43
           What About the Job? 46

Chapter 2 Grief Myths 51
           Give It A Year, You'll Feel Better 53
           When Someone Dies, So Does the
                  Relationship 54
           There Are Stages of Grief for Everyone 55
           Time Heals 56
           Grief, Let's Not Bring It Up 57

Chapter 3	Grief and Guts 59
	Guts for the "Work" 62
	Bereavement Counseling 63
	Remembering 67
	Finding the Guts to Grieve 71
	Forgiveness—Given and Received 73
	Letting Go 74
	Good-Bye Letters 78
	Dating 78
	Onward: Hope on a Rope 80
	A Memorial 81
Chapter 4	Grace—rewards of the work 83
	Freedom No One Wants 86
	Discovering the Woman Within 90
	Looking Inward 91
Chapter 5	Journaling your work 93
	Why Write? 95
	How to Journal 99
	Tools That Help 101
	Things to Remember 101
Chapter 6	Looking Forward 103

Appendix A: Poems that Help 113

Appendix B: Ponder and Reflect on This 121

About the Author 125

Foreword

Loss is universal. Grief is a response to loss. Grief does *not* follow a pattern of clearly defined stages as believed in the past. The death of a loved one can impact grievers emotionally, cognitively, physically, spiritually, socially and behaviorally. On the other hand, loss invites the bereaved to grow through a sometimes winding and spiraling path into a richer life and personhood. How we adapt to and grow through grief is what Joan Broussard calls "the work." Relating what helped to restore her life, she encourages her readers to find a way through the maze of grief into wholeness and freedom.

Though she does not claim to be an expert on grief, Joan is expert on what helped her live and thrive through the losses of her husband Bradley and her parents. In GRIEF, GUTS AND GRACE, she touches on facing some of the everyday practicalities and difficulties of living without a spouse, including buying groceries for one, taking care of home repairs, returning to work and dating again. She gives tips on how to journal and how to seek help. Honest writing and insightful poetry allow grievers, who sometimes have difficulty digesting information, to soak in her wisdom. *The work of grieving is not easy and should be done gently but consistently. With the right support and help from caring and supportive people, our grief can heal with time.*

Scripture proclaims in 1 Corinthians 13:13: *These three remain: faith, hope and love. But the greatest of these is love.* Relationships change, but love does not die. Joan shares that forgiveness and love enhanced her relationship with her husband during his dying and, though doubtful at first, how she discovered and maintains her spiritual connection with Brad. Bravely facing loss and being open to change continue to empower her current relationships and her service to others.

Immense grief ultimately produced GRIEF, GUTS AND GRACE. Joan Broussard found the courage and the perseverance to grow through grief, and she accompanies others as they grapple with their losses. Being a deeply spiritual person, she places her journey and experiences in the grace of God. She inspires her readers to have hope and faith that they, too, will not merely endure but find greater freedom, purpose, and renewed life.

Mary Ristroph Lahey, LPC, LMFT
Director of Bereavement Services
The Center for Loss and Transition
Hospice of Acadiana, Lafayette, LA

Introduction

If you have picked up this book, you have perhaps found yourself a new member of a community of grieving or widowed persons and are now trying to put your life back together and find hope for the future. I joined this community on Wednesday, May 3, 2000, when Bradley, my husband of twenty-nine years, died of a brain tumor. I prayed that day…

> *May 3, 2000–Journal*
> *Lord, my heart and mind are filled with grief at the loss of my husband. I ask that you fill me with the grace to rebuild my life. Please help me to find the guts to stay the course, heal my heart and walk the journey that now lies before me. I know I must do this work if I am ever to be whole again.*

I offer the same prayer for you, dear reader. I know how hard this road is to travel, how lonely it can be even in the midst of family and friends surrounding you with cheerful gestures of love and compassion. They will never truly understand what it's like to lose a partner unless they, too, have experienced that same loss. That is why I have written this book.

After my husband Bradley died, I devoured every book on grief and bereavement I could find. I frantically searched for the answers that would ease my grief and lessen the pain that could take my breath away. I could not foresee a day with any amount of joy. I felt so far removed from the world and the everyday occurrences of people around me that I could not imagine life ever being "back to normal." I knew I had to make some difficult choices. I could allow myself to sink into the pit of depression that was enveloping me or I could seek out a reservoir of strength to survive my loss. From deep within my spirit came the knowledge that all I had to do was find the guts to face my grief, see my loss as part of life's hard lessons, and God would give me the grace to build myself a new, albeit different, life.

"For I know the plans I have for you," declares the Lord, "plans to prosper you and not to harm you, and plans to give you hope and a future."

~Jeremiah 20:11

I know what you're thinking. "This is easy to say, but very difficult to do."

After reading this book, I trust you will be encouraged to take your own look inward and find the guts to face your grief. When you do, I am certain God will honor your effort and bless you with the grace to travel your journey and find joy again. There is one absolute truth I offer to you, my fellow griever; you are not alone on this journey of tears and sadness. Your intimate

God is there right alongside you, even if you are not able to feel God's presence or don't want to communicate with Him. God did not send this loss to you, but He is here with you at this moment, guiding, loving, and carrying you through it. He will show you how to withstand, transcend, and survive your loss, regardless of whether you have lost your husband, wife, child, parent, or close friend.

I'm sure you have heard the old phrase "Give it time, time will heal everything." I want to tell you it is not time that heals; it's what you do with that time that does the healing. The thing you must do if you are ever going to heal is something I call "the work." It is so important to do the work of grieving if you ever hope to be whole and find your new life worth living again. This "work" of grief is different for everyone. My intention in offering you a glimpse of my work is to encourage you not to turn away from doing your own. It's likely to be the most important work of your life. In fact, it may save your life in many ways. It certainly did save mine. Along with my own grief experience, I offer the practical wisdom of many who have gone before—experts in their fields of grief and loss.

What I offer here is not avoidance of the road we are called to travel, just the foretelling of a few potholes. Cracks in the road can't be avoided but are easily negotiated. If we can do this, we conserve our energy for the important job at hand, which is receiving God's grace and finding the guts to face our grief and grow and mend our hearts.

Some of the books I found during my time of grief were *Letter to a Grieving Heart* by Billy Sprague, *Seasons of Grief and Healing, A Guide for Those Who Mourn* by James E. Miller, *It Must Have Been Moon Glow, Reflections on the First Years of Widowhood* by Phyllis Greene, and *Transitions* by Julia Cameron. These books were a great comfort to me. Their inspirational message of courage and strength helped me to look inward and find the guts to recognize God's grace on this journey through grief. There were other helpful books, like *The Wheel of Life, A Memoir of Living and Dying* by Elisabeth Kübler-Ross, *Surviving Grief and Learning to Live Again* by Dr. Catherine M. Sanders, and *Death Where Is Your Sting* by George Maloney. Read as much as you can to better understand the grieving process. These books can help you realize you aren't going crazy.

One of my favorite books, *Widow to Widow* by Genevieve Davis Ginsburg, lists the stages of grief: Shock and Denial, Confusion, Emotional Release, Anger, Guilt, Depression and Isolation, and Recovery. Believe me, you will feel all of these: some more than once, some more intense than others. They won't necessarily come in a particular order and will last as long as it takes. Don't let anyone or anything limit your process. Take as much time as you need to feel your way through your loss.

This book is different from all the others on grief that I've read. In this book you will get advice about what to do when dealing with loss in the day-to-day occurrences that can bring a surviving spouse to his/her knees in an instant.

For example, what to do when you realize the last tube of toothpaste you shared is now empty and you will never share another tube again. Do you sleep on your side of the bed, his side, or in the middle? Find the answer to why you are still buying bananas when you don't even like them. Why is the milk going bad; and then you realize you don't have to buy it in the gallon-size container anymore because there is one less milk-drinker.

The chapters that follow contain my prayers on this journey and how, with the grace of God, I found the guts to face my grief and find my joy again. I offer you some of my personal journaling, which made up my initiation into this community of widows, and how I found the guts to face grief and eventually rebuild my life. Also included is a collection of poems I have written along my journey with grief that has helped me to grow from grief-stricken widow to author, wise to the ways of grief. I trust these poems will be a source of reflection and help you name the hidden feelings that will enable you to be freed, or give voice to a wound you can allow God to heal.

Take your time reading. Be gentle with yourself. If something resonates with you, stay with it, re-read, reflect, and let it sink in to do its work in you. Allow God to speak His wisdom to your heart. Learn, and don't fear "the work." Let the healing begin. All this is offered in a spirit of service and friendship to my community of widowed believers in God's love. I trust these stories will encourage you to take your own look inward and find the guts to face your grief.

When you do, I am certain God will honor your effort and bless you with the grace to travel your journey with a new joy that may be missing in your life.

> *"For I know well the plans I have in mind for you, says the Lord, plans for your welfare, not for woe! Plans to give you a future full of hope. When you call me, when you go to pray to me, I will listen to you. When you look for me, you will find me. Yes, when you seek me with all your heart, you will find me with you, says the Lord, and I will change your lot."*
>
> —Jeremiah 29:11–14

CHAPTER 1

My Grief

Finding My Values

I want to live my life according to my authentic values.
I value honesty–I will be honest.
I value trust–I will be trustworthy.
I value friendship–I will be a friend.
I value solitude–I will be quiet.
I value keeping a promise–I will honor my word.
I value strength of character–I will be true to myself.
I value my faith in God–I will stand faithful amid all things.
It's not that I have a soul, but that I am a soul!
I will find my way and stick to it…
My road, my walk, my life, my heart, my spirit.
I will be loyal to these, to myself.

JOURNALING MY GRIEF

My journey through grief began with the death of my mother, Luda Bernis-Theriot, in 1986. It was my first personal experience of death. It was many years before I could face up to the pain and begin to process my feelings, which I did, using journaling as my primary help. There was no structure to it. I simply wrote out any and all feelings in the journal, but then once I closed the journal, I did not deal with the effects of my loss any further. What is evident through all of my writings is a strong faith in God, who never abandoned me and who loved me through this grief.

I poured out my heart in the pages of my early journals after Mama's death. They were the first of many years of journals that chronicled my faith journey. I had no access to bereavement counselors, a priest for pastoral assistance, or elders with whom I could safely express my feelings. Bradley wrestled for many years with his own feelings of loss as a result of his Vietnam experiences and was not available for these kinds of talks. Also, his law enforcement duties kept him away from home many hours, resulting in limited opportunities for "heart-to-heart" talks that I needed during our marriage.

As a result, my journals became the safest outlet for expression of grief, sadness, and disappointment. Over the years, after the searing pain of losing Mama lessened, I continued to journal, finding within the lines a friend, a confidant, and a most loving God, who taught me the lessons that grief had to teach. Grief would not destroy me if I chose to learn from it. It would provide me with a valuable opportunity to grow. I didn't have Mama to rely on for answers, like how to rescue a botched recipe for crab stew, how to get stains out of my best blouse, a good cure for diaper rash, and even how to mend things after an argument with my husband.

I was faced with looking inward for the strength, for the guts, to face life without her to lean on. Did I have the guts to grow up and not remain in the perpetual "Mama's baby girl" persona that was stifling my own maturity? This grief presented me with a choice: grow up or crumble. I chose the better way, albeit the more difficult. Journaling provided me with the salve for my broken heart to mend and allow my soul to heal.

In October 1999, Bradley was diagnosed with a terminal brain tumor, a glioblastoma multiforme. He underwent brain surgery and extensive radiation treatments. In February 2000, he was accepted into hospice care at the Hospice of Acadiana, the only non-profit hospice in our area. My journals were again my constant companion to express my despair, my emotions, and my total sadness.

It was during the initial visit with the social worker that I was able to name what I had been feeling since his diagnosis just four months earlier—that I couldn't help thinking, dreading, crying, and worrying about what our lives would be like after his death. How could I even have these thoughts when he was still with me and very much alive? I had a chance to talk privately about these feelings with our hospice nurse. Her answer put my mind, my conscience, and my spirit at rest. She also gave it a name—anticipatory grief. I've since heard someone call it "pre-cooked grief." It is the feeling of loss before a death or dreaded event occurs and has been described as a normal process. It's grief that happens when you know there will be a loss, but that loss has not yet occurred. It is the easiest and the hardest to experience. It gives you the opportunity to prepare and take advantage of the time remaining to make the most poignant of memories.

For Bradley and me, this time of grieving opened the doors to honest conversation about our marriage. We talked about the good times as well as the difficult years of our life.

He was able to ask for forgiveness to the grave mistakes he made throughout our marriage. His infidelity was very hard on us. It took me many years to work through my own pain of betrayal and renew a trust in him that we could use as a means of rebuilding our relationship. It did come and we enjoyed a renewed, honest love to the day he died. I am grateful for the grace to have been able to forgive him. Anticipatory grief does offer the chance to resolve any regrets and make amends. Bradley and I used this time wisely. I realize now just how much God was near us, guiding our conversation in asking for and receiving forgiveness. He knew how much this specific aspect of our marriage difficulties would affect me if it was not healed before his death.

I know that anticipatory grief is a normal and important part of coping with the impending death of someone you love. Even though it's rather like being on a roller coaster that won't stop, it can prepare you for the end of life. Your feelings are nothing to feel guilty about. Make the most of every moment you have with your loved one and focus on the positive things, like love, forgiveness, settling old hurts, and making memories.

The hospice staff helped me to realize that for someone in my situation, to anticipate the inevitable was a normal feeling. This knowledge eased my worries and helped me to remember I was not losing my mind, which seemed likely to me much of the time.

Eventually I began to accept the inevitable: my husband was dying, and all I could do was to stand faithful, make him as comfortable as I possibly could, and make memories together. I prayed to God that I would do my best caring for him. In return I begged for only two things: that he would not suffer and that he would always know who I was. I knew there would come a time when his mind would change and he might not recognize anyone, but I desperately hoped he would always know who I was.

I Will Accept

As I watch my husband forget, falter and stumble
I will never let him fall.
My commitment to him is total,
as is my commitment to God.
As I lend myself to my husband,
I lend myself to my God.
I do not understand why this is to be.
And yet I choose to stand faithful, accept and move forward
on this road to "I don't know where."
I do not find myself on this road alone.
My God is with me and whose presence I feel.
He guides me, lest I stumble.
I walk this road in faith.

THE FUNERAL IS OVER, NOW WHAT?

My first week of widowhood was a blur of tears, thank-you notes, phone calls from friends and family expressing sympathy, more tears, and journal writing. I had been journaling for many years, so the privacy of my pages was the safest and most comforting place to go with my grief. After Bradley died, it seemed my journaling took on even greater significance for me. When I was angry about losing Bradley, I was able to express it fully and ultimately see God's presence in my life. My anger was always replaced with the peace of knowing God had His hand on me as I journaled my feelings.

May 22, 2000–Journal
I thank you, God, for this day and for loving me. I can see your grace manifest in my life. It is clear as I look

back on the past months that you carried me and Bradley through every day. Jesus, how can I ever doubt your presence? I never want to doubt you in my life ever again. I want you in my life.

Your will, Lord!

July 17, 2000–Journal

I can't hold my tears tonight. I cry as I write. Lord, this all seems too big to write about. I'm so lonesome for Pookie, I can't stand it. I want him back, then I realize that isn't possible; the pain hurts me so much I think I will smother and my heart will break in two.

Even though I know that you have a plan for my life, Lord, I still ask why, why did it have to be this way? Why couldn't we go on living together? Our marriage was getting so much better. We were just beginning to see our relationship mature.

I feel so angry. I'm mad at you, God, for taking him. I'm even mad at Pookie for dying. All this I know will bring me no peace. I ask you, Lord; create in me a new heart. I want to be at peace with everything that has happened to me. Help me to sort it all out. Please send me your grace.

Be strong and take heart,
all you who hope in the Lord.
~Psalm 31:24

PERSONAL BELONGINGS

My children and I sorted through Bradley's clothes several days after his funeral. I was ready to handle this and asked them to help. We spent a wonderful day sorting his things and talking about the memories we had of him wearing the cowboy boots, the suits, and the ties. I wasn't sure if my son, Macy, would want to wear any of his father's clothes and was so relieved when I heard him say he wanted to wear anything that would fit. He was disappointed when he realized he couldn't wear his father's boots because of their small size.

This sorting process can be very painful for some survivors, so don't begin until you are ready. It helps if you have someone assist you, just to keep you going till the task is complete. They can help you to box and tag things you want to give away and perhaps rearrange your own things to fill the empty space left. I remember putting all my pajamas on hangers on Bradley's side of the closet after we finished boxing his things because I didn't want to see the closet half empty.

LEGAL MATTERS

Then there are the legal matters to attend to; the life insurance, will, and succession of his estate all had to be handled. Macy assisted me with all these things. This can be a particularly difficult time for a widow. Choose someone to help you with these matters whom you trust and who will have your best interests at heart. Take your time, read everything carefully, and don't sign anything until you are certain of every detail and the impact of the document set before you.

Thursday, June 1, 2000–Journal

Good morning, Lord, I'm here sitting at the grave. You told me something in prayer this morning. "I am your partner now. You are not alone." Even though Bradley is gone, that doesn't mean I am alone or without a partner. You are my partner now and always have been. Help me, Lord; remind me always to be faithful to you, my newfound partner, you, Jesus.

Dear Pookie,

I miss you so much—your touch, your hugs, and your kiss. I miss being your wife. I miss belonging to you. I miss having the world know that we are a couple, a team. I have so much to do, and everything seems "too big" for me; especially the succession and insurance business. It's all so scary to me. I pray for Jesus, and you, to help me rebuild my confidence. Why did you have to leave me all by myself? I want to be so angry, but I know it is God's will, not mine, that must prevail. Help me to accept things. I love you, my husband. I wish I could tell you one more time how proud I am, and always was, to be your wife. Rest in peace, my love. I love you, sweetie.

Yours forever,
Tootie.

Since our financial matters were simple, they were handled quickly and without difficulty. Macy accompanied me to the lawyer's office, and I received the final succession papers and signed the final decree on Bradley's estate. It all boiled down to a few sheets of paper and his financial life was over too.

The lawyer was surprised to learn that I had shared our modest life insurance check equally with our two children. He advised that I was not legally obligated to do so since I had legal use of all of our property and was the sole beneficiary of the life insurance. But it felt right to share this with our children, Macy and Sarah. They also received one more reminder of how well their father had taken care of his family, albeit through life insurance. We had never spoken about money before he died, so I wasn't aware of anything special he would have wanted me to do concerning our finances. However, I do feel he let me know that he approved of this.

WAS IT A MESSAGE FROM HIM? YOU DECIDE.

I know there are skeptics out there who say we cannot communicate with the dead. To be honest, I have always been one of them. However, I do not limit God or His power to let us know how we are doing on the journey He sets before us. I have made the choice to believe in the things that some may call coincidence. I prefer to call them personal messages from my intimate God to confirm that I am following the right path and doing the right things to rebuild my life.

One such coincidence happened a few months after Bradley died. My daughter Sarah, her friend Jana, and I went for a much needed getaway at the beach in Gulfshores, Alabama. After an afternoon swim, we decided to go for ice cream.

We were enjoying our cool treat while waiting for the clerk to give me change from the $10.00 bill I'd given to pay for our purchase. When she handed me my change, she said it was the last one-dollar bill she had and apologized for the writing on it.

Initially, I didn't realize the significance of it. I was startled to see that it had the word "Pookie" written in bold letters across the entire bill.

I had been wondering for several days if I had handled the finances and insurance money wisely after Bradley's death. God hadn't delayed with His answer to my prayer. This dollar bill with the word "Pookie" written in large bold letters left me with no doubt. He and I always used our childhood nicknames, Pookie and Tootie, for each other. I choose to believe it was his way of letting me know that sharing the money with our children was the right thing to do. I thank God for such a clear gift of wisdom. Perhaps it was coincidence; however, I believe otherwise. I don't limit God's cleverness to speak to us in a language to fit the moment, the concern. I needed the reassurance about how I had handled the finances, and Bradley's confirmation came on a dollar bill. Just the right language, if you ask me!

LITTLE THINGS AREN'T SO LITTLE

There are other things a new widow is faced with that aren't covered in any of the bereavement books I've read.

Where to sleep: I didn't want to sleep on my side of the bed. I'd look over at his empty side, and my heart would break. So after several nights of sleeping on either side, trying to find "my place," I settled on the middle. It was the spot where we'd meet each other during the night. It seemed to fit best for the first few years. Eventually I changed the king-size bed for a smaller queen-size bed that fit me better so I could sleep on either side or sometimes even crossways.

Toothpaste and mouthwash: It's hard to imagine that insignificant items like a tube of toothpaste or bottle of mouthwash can bring someone to tears for an entire day, but to a new widow it can be a big deal. Bradley and I each had a glass with our toothbrush in it, but always shared a tube of toothpaste throughout our marriage. The day I used the last of the tube of toothpaste Bradley and I had shared was traumatic. It represented to me the reality that I would never share toothpaste with him ever again. It was one of my first opportunities to find the guts to finish the tube and begin a new one, knowing I wouldn't have him to share it with. A little, insignificant thing, but to a grieving spouse, this is big!

*Bananas, milk, and what's for lunch? B*uying groceries for the first time after Bradley's death was one of the most difficult tasks for me. I walked into the local Winn Dixie and started putting bananas in my shopping cart. As I walked over to the apples, I realized I had selected about a dozen bananas for Bradley. I didn't even like bananas all that much. I looked at the rest of the fruits and vegetables and couldn't go on. I had begun my grocery shopping the same way I had for the last 30 years, with someone else's appetite in mind. For the first time in my adult life I didn't have my husband to buy food for, to plan meals for, and to cook for. I couldn't think of a single item I wanted to eat. I left the shopping cart, loaded with bananas, right there in the aisle and left the store. Crying all the way home, I couldn't imagine ever going into a store to shop for myself alone again. When I got home, my daughter Sarah and I worked it out that she would go for groceries for a while until I was able to do it for us. I would still have to overcome this hurdle. And even today I still feel lonesome when I walk in to the grocery store and usually gather up the necessities as quickly as possible and hurry out.

Another thing I couldn't figure out was why the milk kept going bad. Finally I realized I was still buying it in a gallon container, as I had done for years. Sarah and I weren't drinking enough milk to warrant buying it by the gallon any longer. It was heartbreaking to buy a half-gallon container for the first time. I know this is a small thing, but to a new widow the smallest detail can be a huge hurdle to overcome. The good news is that every now and then I do buy a whole gallon of milk, and we drink it up before it goes bad.

Electric blanket: The first winter after Bradley's death was a really cold winter for us here in South Louisiana. I had a good central heating system, and I was rarely cold at night, but once I was sleeping alone again with no one to snuggle up to, the cold night air chilled me even with all the covers I used. Reluctantly, I purchased an electric blanket, which did keep me warm. I cried myself to sleep the first night I used it, settling for artificial warmth instead of the warmth of my husband's body lying next to me.

New paint: The house had not been painted since we'd built it in 1991. I decided to spruce things up a bit and had the bedrooms painted a soft yellow. It was a nice change from the plain eggshell we'd initially used. I really liked it and felt good about selecting a color myself. I fought not to lose my joy when I realized that Bradley would never see the new colors I'd chosen, or any of the changes I was slowly making in the house. This turned out to be one of the first steps in beginning my own life. I was converting our home into my home, one room at a time. With each color change, each furniture change, and each little change in décor, I learned how to find my own original taste in furnishings. I was able to express myself in my surroundings, and it was very liberating. Once I gave myself permission, the house took on a new look, and I became very comfortable in it.

My favorite change was to convert our formal dining room into a library and study. Since we'd only used this room once or twice in the fourteen years we'd been in this house, there weren't very many memories of Bradley being in this specific space, and it wasn't part of the house I associated very much with him. I changed the dining room furniture for a wonderful spacious writing desk, with bookshelves lining an entire wall. Today I absolutely love this room. It is where I'm writing this book, and it is filled with all my favorite things: books I love, pictures, and mementos of my life. As soon as I filled it with my personal belongings, I could go there and not feel as though I was bringing Bradley with me. I used the room as my private place to go and read, write, and remember. I have used it to literally write my way through grief.

HOME MAINTENANCE

Even in the security of our home, my aloneness was overwhelming. It was many months before I was able to refer to our home as "my" home. Taking on many of the small chores that initially felt insurmountable slowly empowered me to emotionally take on the ownership of our home and call it my own. There were many home maintenance tasks that I took for granted when Bradley was alive: the lawn, water pipes in the winter months, and homeowner insurance renewal bills.

And just when you think you've got it all under control, something else will come up to shake your confidence. The first summer after Bradley died; I noticed the air conditioner wasn't adequately cooling the house. I couldn't figure out the cause and was going to call a repairman to check out the system when I found a box of A/C filters in a storeroom in the garage. Bradley had always bought filters by the case and changed them each month. It was then I realized the filter had not been changed since he'd been diagnosed seven months earlier. When I pulled out the filter, all the honey-combed sections were filled with dust, preventing nearly all the return air from getting through. I cried all the way to the garbage to dispose of the old filter.

And then there was the yard. This was the only place I didn't mind handling on my own. I'd always had a housekeeper do the inside cleaning, as I preferred to spend time outdoors. Gardening has always been good therapy for me. My green thumb didn't hurt either. The grounds seemed the least intimidating area to take on alone until I had to mow the lawn for the first time. I couldn't figure out how to operate the large riding mower Bradley had purchased just a year earlier. It was cumbersome and the pedals were hard to reach. Then I made a decision all on my own, thank you very much, and gave the "giant" mower to my son Macy. I went to Sears and sat on several mowers till I found one that was my size and easy to operate. Did you know they make a mower with an automatic clutch? And it was pretty too! I have enjoyed mowing my lawn ever since. Yes, it's my lawn now.

I did have to work out my feelings after the purchase, as Bradley had never liked that particular brand, but I realized I now had to do the yard work, and it was my preference that mattered. This small, perhaps insignificant decision without the consultation of my husband was very liberating.

Just when I thought I had a handle on things around the house, there were some unexpected household emergencies that gave the husband-less a run for her money; like the time I came home from work to find water running down the walls of the kitchen and master bedroom. I frantically called Bradley's uncle Loifey from across the street to help me investigate, and we realized the hot water heater in the attic was leaking. We ran a garden hose up into the attic and drained the 72-gallon water heater. The hot water formed a steamy mist over the entire driveway and looked like a mystical fog. Thanks to some quick thinking, we were able to drain the heater and avoid extensive water-damage repairs.

Managing and caring for your home can be daunting at first, but with a little time, work, and guts, you can choose to do whatever is best for you that will make life easier. These are small victories in this struggle with grief; count them because they are yours. They will prepare you for the bigger decisions you may have to make later.

I do have a word of caution. Don't let things like the A/C filter, yard work, or the hot water heater lead you to think you can't manage the home you and your spouse shared. For some survivors, these challenges can become the catalyst for making a rash and hurried decision to sell their home before being psychologically ready. While it is emotionally draining to handle some of the household chores you never had before, it doesn't mean you can't successfully manage things for yourself with a little help from family and friends. My advice is to wait at least a year before making a major decision about your home if you are able. There usually is a good deal of emotional attachment to the home you shared. Give yourself time to work through your grief and know if and when you are truly ready to leave it.

I gained a lot of confidence as I learned to handle things on my own. I learned that I was not alone, and when I needed help, all I had to do was ask. Family and friends wanted to help. They just didn't always know how to or what was needed. So don't be afraid to ask them. Sometimes the best thing you can do for someone is to let them help you!

WHAT ABOUT THE JOB?

For many widows, having to work after losing a spouse becomes a necessity for economic reasons and is not a choice. Perhaps you are a young widow with children still living at home or you are older and need to supplement an income

Grief, Guts and Grace

from social security. Maybe you've never had to work outside the home, and now you find yourself in a financial situation that requires it. Regardless of the situation, this is a decision that will require some thought. It can be scary to leave the safety of your home and go out into the workplace. The world can feel so big, and no one seems to care about your situation.

Work can be good medicine, but it should never be used as a substitute for paying attention to your grieving heart. Some people choose to hide in their work, which is only a temporary fix. Grief will not be dismissed and will sooner or later catch up to you. So work if you must, to keep your family together. But remember, your grief is work too. It is important to keep them both in perspective. If you have a job to get back to, I would suggest getting back to a normal routine as soon as you are able. Work gave me a place to go every day when I would have otherwise stayed home in bed wallowing in my grief. I needed the obligation to get myself out of the house.

Wednesday, June 28, 2000–Journal

Dear Pookie,

Help me not to be so sad all the time. I feel so alone. I want you back so desperately and yet I know it cannot be. I feel myself accepting the reality more and more each day; but sometimes the lonesomeness is so big that I cannot hold back my emotions. I let them come, cry and feel the pain. I think this is how it should be, feel the pain washing over me and keep moving, somehow.

I am going back to work next week. I think it will be good for me to get back into a routine and be busy. Then I wonder, who is going to call me during day just to see how my day is going, the way you used to? How will I get through the day?

Love,
Tootie

The first day I returned to work, I started to get a little anxious around 9:30 a.m. I began to realize that for the first time in many years, Brad was not going to call at 10:00 a.m. to see how my day was going. When he did call, we usually ended up making lunch plans. But on that day, I received a beautiful bouquet of flowers from my coworkers, and wouldn't you know it was delivered promptly at 10:00 a.m. They had no way of knowing God was using their kind gesture to comfort me and let me know Bradley was thinking of me—at least that's what I chose to believe that day.

It took several weeks before I was able to stay for the entire day. I eventually got back into the swing of my work schedule and received new work assignments, which proved to be very helpful in getting me back into a normal routine. I was fortunate to have a boss who was kind and compassionate. Jamie let me know that if things got difficult I was free to leave and try again the next day. He even gave me time off to attend the hospice bereavement counseling for many months after returning to work.

My at-work family became an integral part of my healing, and the friendships I've made at work are of the lifelong nature. Gail Evans and Beth Leblanc were especially caring and compassionate on days when all I could do was talk about Bradley. You know someone cares when they listen to the same stories over and over without a hint of impatience. These two ladies have walked this grief journey with me. I am forever grateful for their companionship.

The books on bereavement and grief advise widows to get back into life and try to resume a normal routine when they are able. This is good advice. However, they don't tell you how to watch others walk out of the office with their "very much alive" husbands for a lunch date. They don't tell you how to walk through the door at home after being given a promotion and a raise with no one there to share the good news.

You have to learn how to have lunch alone. Going into a restaurant alone is one of the most difficult things I've had to do, but somehow I found the guts to walk into my favorite restaurant and tell the hostess I needed a table for one. God provided the grace for me to enjoy my meal and leave the restaurant with a newfound confidence that I might just be able to make it in this new life of mine. I even enjoy going to the movies alone.

While your hurdle may not be going into a restaurant, you will have to face doing some things alone. Your company isn't so bad. You can learn to enjoy being with just yourself. Look inside and find the guts to face the aloneness, and I promise God will give you the grace to face it and triumph. If you face your grief with God at your center, it cannot defeat you.

CHAPTER 2

Grief Myths

> *"The Lord is your guardian; the Lord is your shade, he is beside you at your right hand. The sun shall not harm you by day, nor the moon by night. The Lord will guard you from all evil; he will guard your life. The Lord will guard your coming and your going, both now and forever."*
>
> —*Psalm 121:5–8*

Many people will want to give you all sorts of remedies and ways to resolve your pain when you grieve. Don't hold it against them. They are only trying to help. Most people aren't quite sure how to deal with grief or the griever. They don't know exactly what to do with you or your pain, so they want to fix it and make it go away—and the quicker the better. But for whom? Here are a few of the misconceptions you may have heard about grieving.

GIVE IT A YEAR, YOU'LL FEEL BETTER

Yeah, right! Our loss will always be our loss. But I can tell you that the searing pain that takes your breath away and can even paralyze you can be an opportunity for change in your life. Once you have lived through the first year of birthdays, holidays, and anniversaries, the pain brought on by these milestones may lessen in its acuteness. We will always honor their memory on these days. It is a lifetime of remembering. For some people the worst of the shock after the first year has passed and they begin to see things more clearly, but whatever your situation, don't let anyone tell you when you are finished grieving. This is your loss, and only you know how you feel.

WHEN SOMEONE DIES, SO DOES THE RELATIONSHIP

Oh, thank God this myth is not true! I believed this for a long time and sorely grieved Bradley's empty chair, his side of the closet, and especially his side of the bed. My relationship with my husband was over, and I stubbornly refused to give it up. I wrestled with God for a very long time, holding on to the role of a married woman who just happened to no longer have her husband. He gently brought me to the awareness that our relationship had not ended; it had simply changed. What an "aha" moment for me! While Bradley was no longer anywhere I could see, touch, or kiss, I could, in fact, feel his presence when I went to prayer and asked for his intercession with God. As I spent the first two years after his death writing his memoir, I had a strong sense of him guiding me to redefine what we now shared spiritually. This relationship was very satisfying in its own way and is a source of great comfort to me still to this day.

THERE ARE STAGES OF GRIEF FOR EVERYONE

Here's another "Yeah, right." Elisabeth Kübler-Ross was the first to present grief as a five-stage adjustment: denial, bargaining, depression, anger, and acceptance. I have read her books and received much insight and healing from her wisdom. We don't all go through these stages the same way, in the same order, or in the same degree of depth.

My experience has taught me that there are as many ways to grieve as there are people. I saw this firsthand with my own children. When Bradley died, my son Macy was 29 years old and my daughter Sarah was 16. They seemed to resume their lives quickly and went back to work and school. I wondered how they had gotten over their loss already when I was still lost, grieving, in great pain, and trying to figure out what to do with my life. Their lives seemed to be back to normal, while mine felt like utter chaos. Of course they had not gotten over their loss so easily.

I quickly accepted bereavement counseling at Hospice of Acadiana and began my grief work. It wasn't until the following year during preparation for Sarah's high school graduation that I saw how grief surfaced in surviving children. As a widow I was acutely aware of Bradley's absence every night going to bed without him and had become somewhat accustomed to his absence. Sarah had become involved in school activities, friends, and a new boyfriend; in a way she had put her grief aside for a time. But a fresh wave of grief began as she realized that her dad would not see her receive her diploma. Another wave of grief was to emerge later as she prepared for her wedding and had to ask her brother to walk her down the aisle instead of her father. There would be new waves of grief later as she gave birth to her first child Brooke, among other life milestones.

Macy experienced his grief in his own way. While Sarah did come with me often to the gravesite for prayer, it was a few years before Macy could manage his feelings of loss enough to come to the cemetery. There were times when he had difficulty coming to the door of our home, knowing his dad would not be there. He has come to terms with the loss of his father, but only after a long, hard struggle with his own grief.

I've learned that for the surviving spouse, grieving happens every day, every minute, every night, and in every intimate detail of a husband/wife relationship that is unique to that tie. If the spouse does their grief work and comes to a place of acceptance, healing can occur. For surviving children, it may come again and again in waves as life events occur and they realize their loss again in the absence of the person they lost.

TIME HEALS

If I had a nickel for every time I heard that one and had not done "the work" of grieving, I would have at least several dollars, a broken, unhealed heart, and a pretty miserable life. It does take time for our wounds to heal. Sometimes it feels like the pain of our loss will go on forever. I remember a time about a year after my mother died when I began to ask God, "Will this pain last forever? When will it ease up and not hurt so badly?" It seemed by the time I was able to articulate this question for myself, the pain was actually easing somewhat. The work of grieving is not easy and should be done gently but consistently. With the right support and help from caring and supportive people, our grief can heal with time.

GRIEF, LET'S NOT BRING IT UP

I agree, it did make me sad, but mixed with that sadness was the need to talk about it. I wanted to talk about my life with Bradley and especially to talk about his last days. The silence was deafening and very isolating. For many people, there is healing in telling our story of grief. Giving witness to our experience of losing someone significant provides a source of strength to continue the grieving process. It becomes one more layer of our wound that receives the healing salve our hearts need to look to the future. By coming to terms with our past, we are able to be fully present, see who we want to be, and begin our new life with hope.

CHAPTER 3

Grief and Guts

What Our Eyes Have See

We have seen it.
We have tasted it.
We have reveled in it.
These souls connected by loss,
help each other look beyond what we have seen.

We have seen devotion without concern for self.
We have seen service to another no matter the fatigue. We have
seen hearts soften, souls refreshed.
We have seen life at its fullest and cruelest.

We have seen a part of us become something we no
longer recognize, ravaged by illness.
Some of us are not sure what it is exactly we have seen,
while others are quite certain and give witness to it eagerly.

We have seen God's hand touch a soul we thought untouchable, and yet
they heard His whispered secrets of their journey home.
We have seen those we love make the transition from this place to
the next, God's home.
We have tasted this bittersweet food we call grief;
the aftertaste of love shared with someone who is no more.

GUTS FOR THE "WORK"

How do you know when you have enough guts to begin this grief work? I wish I could tell you the precise moment when you receive adequate strength to do this sacred work. There is no magic wand to fill you with the energy and courage to begin. What I can tell you is that perhaps one day you may notice you feel better than the day before. You might perceive it as an indication that you have already begun this work. You may wake up one day and feel tired and sad about feeling tired and sad…this could be another indication that you may already be "working."

Actually, finding the guts to do the work is more of a surrendering to it. There is a final acceptance of the reality of the death of your loved one and the pain it brings. You have adjusted to the new environment of your surroundings, and perhaps, like me, you have found your new place in the center of the bed rather than sleeping on your side or theirs. It's a small thing, but a matter of acceptance just the same.

You realize that the pain of your loss is still there, but it might be somewhat muted and not as swift or razor sharp—a sign that you have been doing the work. For me, it was the realization that I was beginning to look forward to a weekend trip with the kids or a shopping trip with friends. It was a glimmer of sunshine in an otherwise gloomy outlook on everything around me. This anticipation was the first indication that I had been doing my grief work and healing was taking place.

BEREAVEMENT COUNSELING

As my work of grieving continued, I learned to answer its call and not ignore it. When I ignored my feelings, it seemed I'd fallen into a hole and couldn't find my way out. That's when I learned just how much strength and guts it takes to do this work. If I was willing to face my grief, climb out of the hole, God would bless me with the grace to begin healing.

Bereavement counseling was a tremendous help to me, and I recommend it to anyone who is grieving. It's important to work through any unresolved issues with an experienced professional counselor. Talking about serious issues with family and/or friends can sometimes do more harm than good. While they mean well, some people may encourage you to get on with your life before you are ready or to make decisions you are not emotionally prepared to make. Finding the guts to deal with your grief is difficult, and having the assistance of a professional bereavement counselor to help navigate the grief process can be invaluable.

If you decide to pursue counseling, contact your local hospice agency, church, or hospital. Many of them have grief centers or bereavement programs for widowed persons. These are usually run by professional, compassionate people who typically have group sessions that are very helpful. You will benefit from these programs and make new friends who will totally understand your feelings. You will soon see that you aren't alone.

Bradley was cared for by the staff of Hospice of Acadiana in Lafayette, Louisiana, for three months before his death.

Part of their program is bereavement counseling for survivors. My bereavement counselor was caring and compassionate to all of us attending the grief support group sessions looking for support and guidance. I attended these sessions for thirteen months after Brad's death. The people in the group I started with are still some of my dearest friends. We helped each other through the most difficult times of our lives and formed a bond that won't easily be forgotten.

> ***August 8, 2000–Journal***
>
> *Hospice support group was really good today. It is such a safe place to be honest about my feelings. I am facing my anger and feel it being replaced by forgiveness. Anger is such a destructive emotion. It stifles growth and progress and confuses everything. It gets in the way of really feeling and finding the guts to face my grief. I refuse to allow it to control*
>
> *me. I turned and looked at it in the face today. Bernie said when I had the courage to look right at it; I should ask it for my gift. I wanted to laugh at her suggestion. But before I knew it, I realized what the gift was: forgiveness. My love, my Pookie, I give this gift to you, my forgiveness. Please find a way to tell me you feel my love and my forgiveness, for it is real and total and mixed with my tears.*

There is a bond created when we look at the world through the same sad eyes, share our grief stories, our tears, and our hope for the future. You can't compare your grief to anyone else who is grieving. As one wise grieving woman once said, "We compare our insides to other people's outsides and we never measure up.

It's like comparing apples to oranges."

We don't grieve the same; however, I discovered that the group who attended bereavement counseling together had something in common. When I came in for our sessions, I would mention being "in the hole" when I had experienced a painful weekend. The others in my group took up the name as well. One person might come in and share, "I was in the hole all weekend; thank God I made my way out of it." Another might say, "Knowing I was coming to our group helped me to get out of the hole easier."

The Hole

We call this place the hole, a place of pain, sorrow and certainly tears; this is a place of remembering.

We try to avoid its business, its pull to spend time in its dreary yet healing depths; not wishing to step into this chasm of memories, lost love, loneliness and the unresolved.

Should you dally and not heed the call to this place, it will come to you, at a time when you don't expect it. There is no avoiding this place for those of us hearing its beckoning. This place, this hole, this grief is ours, and no one can put things in order here but us.

We take from this place only the things that will mend our battered lives, leaving there the grief of a love whose season has passed. And for those who are brave enough to answer the call to this place, they learn its secret.

Once you allow yourself to go into it and see all the things from the past, feel the feelings of the present and take off the masks of falsehoods and the unresolved, you can come out of this hole whole and with a new courage to face life again.

You will come out of this place forever changed and better able to see the gifts you carried out as you emerged from this place we call the hole.

The support we received really helped us maneuver our way in, out, and around this "hole" of grief. Whenever someone was having a particularly rough time, they would refer to it as "time in the hole". It became a name we all used. Some days we were glad that we recognized when the "hole" needed some attention and when we were able to navigate in and around it as well as not to fall in too deep. Other days were happier when someone recalled being able to climb out of the hole and was feeling stronger for it. These days were filled with many tears; some happy, some sad. Many stories of our loved ones were shared. Always, there was encouragement from one to the other.

REMEMBERING

It was always comforting to remember some of the intimate moments Bradley and I shared. There was a day that held a moment I asked God to save in my mind for a day when my heart would need its healing gift. Sometimes a memory can take on a life of its own, and this one has for me. It was a moment so tender and delicate and yet so vivid and strong. It has not been diminished by time and has become a gift. This memory presents its gift of feeling, circumstance, and detail that sustains me in times of sadness. Many things can be said without words. A simple touch, a kiss, a hug can speak volumes about love, especially a love that is changing. It was a day full of harsh reality. Bradley was sitting at the bedside, his legs weakening as the illness robbed his strength and our future. We hugged, we kissed, and we held each other in an embrace that seemed like it could last forever. While being held in his arms, I prayed with all my might to a God who I was beginning to know in an intimate and powerful way.

January, 2000–Journal
"Oh Lord, put the memory of this hug we shared today in the category of ones to last forever, never to be forgotten, or diminished even slightly by the passing of time. It must be my hug to remember when he is no longer here to hold me."

I welcome the gift this moment still has for me. I wanted this sweet, precious moment to be seared into my memory. I knew Bradley's days were short and wanted to savor this intimate moment with him while he was lucid enough to share it with me. This intimacy would have to sustain me in my time of grief to come. This memory of a love whose season was over much too soon but is still alive in this hug to last a lifetime. I can still remember it all in every detail, the feeling, the touch. I am grateful for this memory gift. In those days when grief and absence seemed unbearable, I was able to bring myself back to that day and allow the hug to caress and comfort; my prayer being answered. And in that moment, time can stand still and the memory presents its gift.

GRIEF, GUTS AND GRACE

Holy Tears

Let them approach and let them in.
Let them have their way.
Let them come in full, running over.

They will come slowly, sweeping over you like a gentle
mist, covering every hurt, every burden.
They will come with a purpose and intended meaning; like a father on
his way to help and comfort his child.

Like healing water, reaching your soul's driest places.
The gift of tears has the ability to make all things hurtful
fall to a place of clarity and proportion.
As you welcome this gift, life is renewed and
the sting of heartache is soothed.
Like salve for the soul; healing and refreshing.
Let them come.

The gift of holy tears brings with it the potential for new
beginnings each time you indulge them.
Let them be your companion.
Allow them entrance to the secret places never before explored.
Allow them to do their intended work.
Let them come.

Thank you, Lord, for the gift of my tears.
They are companion to my memories.
As I remember, they come, wash my heart and heal my grief.
Thank you for the mercy in my healing tears.

FINDING THE GUTS TO GRIEVE

Thursday, August 3, 2000–Journal

Well, my love, a milestone for us today; three months. I pray that you are happy, worry-free and filled with God's love. I know that you are because tears come just as I write these words. They feel like tears of confirmation that you are nearby, with Jesus and all the angels. I bet you are singing like you used to in your high school chorus class.

Oh how I miss you so. I wore our rings today, to honor our milestone. I let them remind me that you are always with me. Your memory will always be alive in my heart. You are such a part of me. There are times when I say something that sounds just like you. Or I'll do something in the same manner you did.

I want to keep myself, my heart, my soul open to hear from you. Tell me somehow that you are okay and well and happy. And look, as I sit on the swing outside writing these lines, hoping you can reach me, I look up and right there in front of me, a dove walking in the grass, not ten feet away. It's a mourning dove, gray with black specks on its wings. The dove is just standing there, looking out toward me, not moving. I thought the motion of my swinging would frighten him off, but no. And now look, a large red cardinal just landed on the birdbath, just a few feet from the dove. The dove hasn't moved. It's just sitting, moving its head from side to side. For at least 15 minutes I've enjoyed the dove's company. I choose to believe God can speak to us through nature. Thank you, Lord.

After Bradley's death, I began to search out my own identity. I was no longer Mrs. Broussard. Much of that role identified my world. Now that this role didn't exist for me, I struggled to know myself. I was no longer one of a pair, a couple. This new season in my life brought with it the challenge to fly solo. I wanted to soar on the wings I had grown together with him. God was teaching me to use these new wings.

The Pair

We were a pair, a couple to the world.
There was always a "ying" for every "yang" a "wic" for every "wac".
One who washes and one who dries.
Without either one, the pair is no more.

At times when the two sides collided, discord followed.
Love was constant and ready to meet the challenge of the discourse.
Love was the sustaining meal that fed life to the pair.
The pair burst forth into a love that gave wings to each.

And when the pair had learned to fly in perfect union
and harmony—they parted.
No longer a pair; each to his own path.
This new season brings with it the challenge to fly solo.

I soar on wings I have grown together with someone special. I reach
new heights on the memories that sustain my flight.
For not to fly would mean nothing was learned,
and no one was loved.

FORGIVENESS—GIVEN AND RECEIVED

As we work through our grief and are able to tell our stories, things of the past come up and beg for our attention and reconciliation. Before we embark on new beginnings, we may need to give forgiveness, ask for forgiveness, and release the things that burden our heart and prevent our forward movement. As I looked at my life with Bradley, I began to see things clearly and started to ask myself, "If I could change the past, would I?" As with most marriages, we'd had our ups and downs. I wondered if I could change the past, would I? After all, it comes together to make up my life experience. There were some things I wanted to ask forgiveness for:

Forgiveness

Forgive me for not always putting you first.
Forgive me for wanting more from you than you could give.
Forgive me for not meeting your needs, or telling you of mine.

Forgive me for not building you up as much as I could have.
Your child within suffered as a result of my neglect.
You were always my hero, I should have told you.

Forgive me for being tired and wanting our struggle,
and your illness to be over.
Forgive me for anything I missed to make you more comfortable.
Forgive me for any impatience you felt from me in my fatigue.

It wasn't till Bradley was leaving me to be with God that I realized how precious he truly was. Only God could give me this insight, and I am grateful to have received it. My lesson in unconditional love did come. I learned to love unconditionally and without reservation, forgiving all hurt and pain. So there is my question: If I could change the past, would I? No, I would not change a thing. Our life together was as it was supposed to be, filled with love, rocky roads, passion, and a strong dedication to each other.

LETTING GO

My first step in letting go and accepting my loss was on Bradley's first birthday in heaven. It would have been his 51st birthday. I realized that anticipating something is usually much worse than when the event day finally arrives. I fretted about what the day would be like, his birthday without him. It was like planning for a party, all the while knowing the honoree was never going to show up. I thought I would stay home, curl up with my memories, and have a private party with just his memory and me in attendance.

As the day grew nearer, I began to figure ways of avoiding it. Rather than take the day off, I went into the office. However, by mid-morning, the memories were like the tide that recedes back into the depths, hidden from conscious memory but now flowing slowly and steadily higher to fill the nooks and crannies of the rocky shore that surrounded my grief-stricken heart. I knew there was no way to avoid this high tide of memories, and my grief companion, God, was bringing me to a place where I could celebrate this day in His intended way. I have always tried to discern when God was speaking and giving me instruction for my life. This day, I knew it was His voice I heard: "Find the guts to face this, and I will give you the grace to see it through. I will be with you."

By lunch time, I had finished the work I'd halfheartedly started that morning, and then told the girls in the office I was going home and left for the day. Somehow as I got into my car, I knew exactly where I was going. I went home, picked up my journal, the 8x10 picture of Bradley and me, and a large box of tissues.

This was the first time I thought to bring a picture of him with me when I went to the cemetery. I wondered why I hadn't thought of this before. I'd been having difficulty remembering him as the strong, lean, handsome man I so loved before the cancer took its toll on his appearance. Anxiously I gathered up my essentials and headed for the cemetery. As I walked up to his grave with tears already starting to flow, I sat on the bench and rearranged the flowers I'd brought earlier in the week.

As I opened my journal and began to write, I realized with the utmost clarity that at this moment Bradley was exactly where he was supposed to be and so was I. The realization that hit me was profound. This was as much time as we were ever supposed to have together, not a moment more or less. May 3, 2000 was always to be the last day of Bradley's journey in this world as an individual and as a couple with me. We taught each other many things, and now it was time for each of us to go on, albeit in separate directions.

Seedlings of Surrender

It's your first birthday in heaven.
Sweet memories keep me strong amid the loneliness of grief.

Our spirits intertwined still, our hearts joined like the day we met. Still dancing as in our youth; still dancing like the two rings of gold now dangling around my neck.

I sit at the grave with my essentials: journal, pen and your picture to wake up memories that are lost in the forest of my grief and I find the gift I want to give to you — release.
And yet, it's my own releasing I receive.

It is my love for you and desire for your happiness that I hand you over to the Father; to be at His party in full attendance with no tugs from here trying to get you back in a moment of desperate longing for one more memory.

As I leave the grave, having gathered up my essentials,
I know I have been the one receiving a birthday gift.

Brad was now to receive the glory of God in heaven and enjoy the company of Jesus for eternity. For me, I believe I am to go on to live in this world knowing that I have shared many years with a very special soul, and for that I am grateful. I have been taught many lessons from God via my life with this man. It is now up to me if I choose to use what I have learned wisely and in service of others. I cannot say that it is easy. It takes guts to face my aloneness, look to the future, and remember that I am not alone. The grace of God in my life makes it worth living, and I am on my way to a new life.

GOOD-BYE LETTERS

Write as many good-bye letters to your loved one as you need to. I've written several, as the need to say good-bye one more time comes up for me. It may take many letters to address all of the unspoken issues that weigh on your heart. Don't allow fear to rob you of the healing that can occur in the writing out of all the things you wish you had said to your loved one.

You might even try being silent for a while, and then write the letter your loved one wants to write to you.

DATING

I received my first advice about being a widow and dating from an unexpected source. It came about two weeks after Bradley died. My father called early in the morning to see if I had any plans for the day. When I told him I didn't have anything to do, he asked if he could come over. He sounded intent on something I couldn't identify, so I invited him to come right away.

He had been a widower for a relatively short time. He and my stepmother Ella married less than two years after my mother died. I realize now that he was lonely and needed someone to share his life with. At 67 years of age, it was difficult to face the long days and even longer nights alone after spending so many years with my mother. His mission on this day was to share a lesson in grief with his newly widowed daughter that he'd learned firsthand.

He arrived a short time later, and we sat at my kitchen table, drank coffee, and made "small talk" until the tears filled his eyes. He said he wanted to talk to me about something important. The feelings he had been holding just beneath the surface couldn't be held back any longer. They gave way and he allowed the sobs to escape without restraint.

My tears joined with his as I asked him, "Daddy, how will I get through this? How did you do it back then when Mama died?"

He answered, wiping his face, "Oh Tootie, it's not easy. Sometimes, it's like it was just yesterday. You feel like you can just go crazy sometime." We agree and share more tears. "Tootie, there's something I want to tell you. Just go slow. Don't go too fast."

I wasn't clear as to his meaning or what it was that he wanted me to go slow about, and I told him so.

"You know, it's lonesome when you're by yourself. But don't go too fast. You know, it's like when you have a wagon with two mules pulling it. The two mules pull that wagon together for a long time, and they each pull their share of the load evenly and neither one goes faster than the other. But then, when one of those mules is gone, you think you have to hurry and get a new mule. Tootie, listen well. That new mule will never, never pull like the first one!"

More tears, sobs, and I reached over the table, and we shared a long hug of understanding. Then he continued, "Just remember, don't go too fast. It's going to be hard, but go slow and take your time. You have your children and your little grandson to keep you busy. Let them and the rest of the family help you. Just don't jump too fast."

Although my father was not an educated man, his wisdom was sound. The words of this 81-year-old Cajun father may not have been the most eloquent, but the message was clear. Although he did go on with his life after my mother's death, he knew the love they shared could not be duplicated. His advice to take it slow and not make any decisions too quickly was sound.

My life may have seemed empty and alone, but it was up to me to have the guts to find my joy within and not look to fill it by rushing into a relationship that I was not ready for.

Don't trust your emotions at this time; they are not reliable and may lead you to do something you may regret later when a clearer head and heart will be present.

ONWARD: HOPE ON A ROPE

Six months after Bradley died, my father died. I remember asking my bereavement counselor at Hospice of Acadiana, "Do I have to start all over again?" She held me carefully and said it was up to me. What I learned is that grief is bigger than me. As I grieved I grew and became bigger than my grief. So when the next loss came, sooner than later, I was bigger and stronger than before. This second grief did not overwhelm or overcome me. I didn't look away from it. I had gained the courage to look at it and begin "the work" from a stronger, wiser center.

During the course of "Journaling through Grief" and working with people in Spiritual Direction, I have learned to walk alongside people who are actively grieving and doing "their work." The key is not to lead or drag them. It's their grief, and I am with them on this road to wholeness. I am present and allow them to lead the way, giving support, a listening ear, and hope.

A MEMORIAL

In honor of your loved one, you may want to make a donation to your church or local civic organization in their name. This is a very good way to leave a legacy for future generations to remember. I was able to facilitate the building of a Labyrinth Garden and provide funds for the Bereavement Program at Hospice of Acadiana in Lafayette with a raffle in Bradley's name. The raffle was conducted by the booster club of our local minor league hockey team, the Louisiana Icegators.

Bradley and I had always purchased season tickets and rarely missed a game. In the last months before his death, as Bradley and I sat together, he watched as I cross-stitched the

Icegators logo. It was during the hours of sitting together, watching these stitches take shape, that we had talks about our life together and the love we shared. As his illness progressed he began to think he was stitching it with me. He would ask me how "his stitching" was coming along.

When I started this cross-stitch piece during the summer before the 1999-2000 season began, my original intent was to give it to the Icegator organization for getting to the Kelly Cup finals. As fate would have it, I didn't get to finish it then.

I completed it after his death and then decided on a new purpose for it. The kind and compassionate people at Hospice of Acadiana helped our family during the last months of Bradley's life. I gave them the cross-stitch piece to raffle and asked that the proceeds be donated to Hospice of Acadiana for their care of Bradley and the rest of our family.

We raised $12,000 in this raffle. The money was donated in January, 2001 to Hospice of Acadiana. Most of it was used to construct a Labyrinth Garden, where there is a plaque with Bradley's name on it. When we walk the Labyrinth, it fills my heart with joy to see his name there for the world to see as a witness to his life.

I have been volunteering for Hospice of Acadiana since Bradley's death on their Speaker's Bureau, plant sale, television telethon, and United Way campaign.

You too may find an organization that helped you the most and offer your services as a volunteer. It will help to fill some lonely hours, and you will meet new people and make new friends. It will take guts to step out of the house and do this, but I promise it will be worth it.

CHAPTER 4

Grace—rewards of the work

Change Is My Teacher

Change tells, teaches and promises.
There it is, telling, every day and most truthfully every night;
You are alone.
This change has taken away the part of you that you thought made you whole.

It teaches that pain is part of happiness.
It teaches how someone physically ravaged by disease can be renewed spiritually and emerge a new soul. It teaches about the endurance of the human spirit and the strength of memories.

And finally, it promises that life is worth living and is self-renewing.
Life does have a purpose, even in the face of death.
One has only to be open to the possibility. It promises that once change has occurred,
a new path is laid and life can be good again.
It promises that as God's creation, we do have the capacity to live and love again.

Yes, change tells, teaches and promises.

FREEDOM NO ONE WANTS

It's a freedom that comes by way of heartache, pain, and loss. It's the freedom to volunteer for causes that now mean a lot to you. It's the freedom to choose the life that you want. In doing this "work" I discovered the woman I had stifled for many years. She was afraid to show herself to a world that was now so different without Bradley.

I know you, like me, would never feel or even verbalize that you are grateful or happy that your loved one died. The freedom I am referring to is the freedom to make choices for yourself perhaps for the first time in your life, the freedom to do things, see places in the world that you've always dreamed of. It may be a time to make all your hidden dreams come true, with your loved one in the heavenly place to encourage you. Pray and ask for the assistance you need from God to help open up the world to new adventures not possible before.

This new freedom was intimidating for me at first. I found myself free to volunteer, visit family and friends, and even pursue further education. It is certainly not true to say that my life with Bradley was not fulfilling. It was. However, in a relationship, there is always compromise, and my portion was to be a working mom who didn't have many interests or friends outside of work. God blessed me during my working years with wonderful, caring coworkers, who remain my companions to this day. It wasn't until after Bradley died that I was able to expand these relationships outside of work.

Early in my marriage, I left dreams of higher education behind and made a wonderful life with my husband and children. But now, without that relationship and its compromise to hold my dreams and desires in their place, I find the world to be available to me in a brand-new way.

What would I do with all my time? I recall the day when this freedom became real. I was asked to do some volunteer work for Hospice of Acadiana, the agency who cared for Bradley during his illness. As I considered my answer, I realized that I could actually say yes to them without having to consider my husband's reaction. Around that time I was asked to participate in a United Way campaign video as a recipient of services from Hospice of Acadiana. I told my son Macy about the opportunity, but with a sense of sadness, I realized the price I had paid for the freedom to do it. In his wisdom, he comforted me with the words, "But Mom, it's not a price, it's a reward for always taking such good care of Dad and us." His words were a huge affirmation that I truly deserved the new life that lay before me.

I eventually did recount my experience for the Hospice of Acadiana on the United Way video that year. I also worked on the Hospice Speaker's Bureau, and I continue to volunteer in the Bereavement Department giving Journaling through Grief workshops. I still love this work and feel much gratitude as I sit with people who are just beginning their own work of grieving.

I first talked about this freedom with a group attending the Journaling through Grief series that I presented at Hospice of Acadiana. I am always amazed at the expression on their faces when I bring up the subject: "Now I can do whatever I want." Eyes light up and connections are made. It's the freedom they already know but have been afraid to verbalize.

Perhaps they have been in a stifling relationship with a spouse who limited outside activities as mine did. I see that "I know just what you mean" expression on their faces. There were some who were married for many years and had not been able to chase after dreams, but now spoke about going back to college, taking cruises, yoga classes, doing volunteer work that they never would have done within the confines of their marriage. This is not to say their lives were not full and happy. Marriage and children are the ideal for most people, and for some it means willingly putting the dreams of their youth on the shelf.

At that point, my time was my own, my finances were secure, and my life was mine to live as I chose. The discovery of this personal freedom to chase after my dreams and ideas was very liberating, and, I must admit, scary too.

I've heard many stories that illustrate this newfound freedom experienced by the surviving spouse. This freedom takes on a variety of appearances. For instance, one woman told her children that she wanted to go out and buy the most expensive rump roast she could find for a family meal. They couldn't understand why she wanted to be so extravagant with this purchase, as their parents had always been very frugal.

But it had been the father who had never wanted to spend too much, and now that she was free to shop for groceries without the censure of a frugal husband, she could buy and cook a cut of meat she had always wanted. This freedom gave her the courage to make this purchase and enjoy it. The gift of this freedom was that it came with no guilt. She had been doing her grief work and was becoming truly free.

For another grieving spouse who found herself financially secure for the first time with the help of life insurance benefits, traveling to places she'd dreamed of as a young woman became a reality. With the freedom of time and resources, she was able to fulfill those long-held dreams and was taking her children with her.

There were those surviving spouses who enjoyed a variety of freedoms: from having to ask permission to go shopping, buying a new dress, or simply not cooking dinner and having ice cream instead. One widow expressed pleasure in being able to drink directly from the milk carton with no one to judge her manners. Some changed their home décor to reflect their own personal taste, while others changed their housecleaning routine to suit themselves rather than a fastidious spouse or even hiring cleaning help to do it. To some, these may seem of no big importance, but to the one left behind, discovering these little "big freedoms" marks the beginning of new life and healing.

I am filled with gratitude to help you, dear reader, learn that you do have the guts to do your grief work and can survive it. My life gives witness to that. It is my prayer that you will do the same for those who come after you.

DISCOVERING THE WOMAN WITHIN

There came a time when I realized I had been doing the work of grieving my loss and I was ready to embrace life again. But I had questions: *Who am I exactly? What have I learned from this experience?*

This Woman Is Me

I miss being a couple with you.
And who is this one of a pair that used to be?
A woman who is strong, yet needs someone to lean on.
She is faithful, yet questions.
She is resilient, yet wavering in the midst of her grief.

She is me, with all my wics and wacs, zigs and zags,
with my lil' girl naivety and tenderness as well as my sometimes hardheaded attitude.
She is me, with all her experiences forging this woman to be.

This woman I am getting to know from the inside out.
This woman I am growing to admire and respect.
This woman I am proud to introduce to others.

This woman has the courage and guts to unmask
any false trait, and face past memories.
This woman who I love and whose company I am pleased to keep.

LOOKING INWARD

This work of grieving involved looking inward and finding the willingness to allow God to do His work. We must be still and let Him heal our woundedness. As we heal and regain our strength, life can be good again. Hope for a brighter future can be found.

As you heal and begin to look to the future with new eyes, take some time to decide what you really want out of this new life of yours. It is my humble prayer that you will receive the help you need as you journey on with hope. If you can find the guts to do your work of grieving, to remember your experiences and the lessons they have to teach, you may be able to allow God to heal your broken heart and receive the grace He has for you. The choice is yours.

CHAPTER 5

Journaling your work

WHY WRITE?

We all pray for spiritual growth and have a desire for a closer relationship with God, which may be part of the reason you picked up this book. He wants an intimate relationship with us, not just a casual one where we meet for just a short time on Sundays, say a few prayers, and we've done our duty for the week; or when we are in the deep pain of grief and don't know where to turn.

To heal wounds and begin to grow spiritually, we could just say the prayers we were taught as children. They are beautiful and I believe God wants us to use them to call on Him. However, these words were given to us by others to talk to God. I believe God wants to hear our prayers, our petitions, and our praise, in our own words. He especially wants to hear about our pain, suffering, and grief.

I grew up saying prayers that I'd learned in religion classes taught by the nuns in a local Catholic school. Much of my childhood image of God was formed as a result of fear; fear of punishment and judgment. My catechism teachers didn't present God as a loving, caring God as much as they taught us He was a punisher of our sins. As a result, I learned to be afraid of Him and developed an image similar to that of the Wizard of Oz…unapproachable and to be feared and certainly not my intimate God.

In my late 20s, I accepted Jesus as my Lord and Savior and began to see and feel His love. My childhood image was replaced with an intimate and loving God who cared about me. He was always understanding and forgiving, no matter how good or how bad I was. He never disappointed me, and His love for me is the one thing in this life I know I can count on never to change.

I began writing my prayers in 1983 in my own words mostly because there were more things I wanted to say to God and they weren't in my prayer books. My journaling then was very simple. I was spiritually immature, and most of my writing asked God for something. When I heard about someone who was ill, I prayed for them in my journal. When problems arose in my marriage, at work, or with family or friends, I would come to my journal and ask God to fix them or fix the problem. I expressed my anger, my frustration, my hurt, my happiness, and my joys. I cried, laughed, screamed, and hollered in the safety and comfort of my pages.

After a while, I began to notice that many of the things I'd written about in my journal had either been resolved or were just not troubling me any longer. The situation may not have changed, but I had. I felt different after writing. I realized that God must have been working with me to change my spirit and my attitude toward the situation I'd written about.

My image of God had changed. He had been the "mean Wizard" of my childhood, but He was my intimate God now, not to be feared, but loved; and He loved me back. I began to see that my writing was really my praying. As I continued to pray this way, I was able to see God's hand in my life each day because I was focused on looking for Him.

When my mother died in 1986, my journals became a place to express my grief. I missed her and still needed her wisdom and guidance. I talked to God about the changes I needed to make from being "Mama's baby girl" to a mature woman who could face life without her to lean on. As a result, I learned to lean on God.

Then when my husband Bradley died in May 2000, I used my journal to work through my toughest grief yet. Coming to terms with losing him, learning how to be a widow, taking care of a house, and building a new life for myself, again I leaned on God by writing it out.

Then six months later when Daddy died, I again used my prayer journal to express my feelings of being an orphan at the age of 48. God showed me that He was the only constant in my life. People were leaving me, but He wasn't.

Yes, my image of God has changed over the years, and I feel very close to the God I know and love today. By utilizing journaling I have been able to go back over the weeks, months, and perhaps years and read about God loving me, blessing me, and healing me.

If we have the guts to come to terms with the losses we have experienced, we can allow God to love us and heal our broken hearts. He can bless us with His grace. Journaling our experience helps to process the lessons we are learning. Journaling our feelings while grieving provide a safe outlet to express the wide range of emotions that come up after the loss of a loved one. There are feelings of anger, sadness, and even despair that can be expressed on the pages of a journal.

It has been my experience that these feelings lose much of their power to stifle my healing after I have released them on the page.

One of the many benefits of journaling comes from God. He can give us a revelation or insight to a burden we are carrying. At the moment we may not see much meaning in it, but if we use reflective writing to record it, at some later time while re-reading it, the meaning may become clear and the whole matter will perhaps make perfect sense to us. Had we not journaled the experience, the lesson would go unlearned.

Another benefit of journaling is that it can help to clarify what we see, hear, and feel. After the death of a loved one, even the little things can be difficult and our memory can be foggy. If we write down the things we see, hear, and feel, they can become more focused and the path we are to take or decisions to make clearer. We journal to process our grief and the lessons it teaches.

God even recommends that we write down our experiences. He instructs Habakkuk to record the results of his prayer.

> *I will stand at my guard post, and station myself upon the rampart, and keep watch to see what he will say to me and what answer he will give to my complaint. Then the Lord answered me and said "Write down the vision clearly upon the tablets, so that one can read it readily. For the vision still has its time, presses on to fulfillment and will not disappoint. If it delays, wait for it. It will surely come, it will not be late."*
>
> *Habakkuk 2:1-3*

John, author of Revelation, was given a vision by God. He heard God tell him to write down what he saw.

> *I was caught up in spirit on the Lord's Day and heard behind me a voice as loud as a trumpet, which said, "Write on a scroll what you see and send it to the seven churches."*
>
> *Revelation 1:10-11*

The disciple Luke expresses the need for writing things down so that we can be clear about what we are learning and the healing we receive.

> *I too have decided, after investigating everything accurately anew, to write it down in an orderly sequence for you, most excellent Theophilus, so that you may realize the certainty of the teachings you have received.*
>
> *Luke 1:3-4*

HOW TO JOURNAL

The first thing is to take some time to reflect on your writing; notice what feelings you had about what you wrote and the experience of writing it. After your time of writing, stay there and think about the stirrings, the inner movements of your spirit. Do they cause you to turn toward God or away from God? Notice your physical sensations. Are you more relaxed, feeling peaceful, or are you tense, feeling challenged by something that came up as a result of your writing?

Recognize that when you write, you are not alone (just like when you pray). God is there holding the pen with you, guiding you, teaching you, loving and healing you. Writing about our lives, our experiences (past and present), opens us up to the grace God has for us. It allows Him to come in and help us better understand those circumstances.

Oh, I know we will never fully understand why things happen in our lives. But we can come to accept the things we cannot control or comprehend. Our journal is the place to set those issues and feelings down in the safest place…the heart of Jesus.

By developing the practice of journaling, you will be able to go back over the weeks, months, and perhaps years and read about God loving you, blessing you, teaching you, and most of all, and healing your grieving heart. If you have any doubts that He has been walking with you through your life, just go back and read some of your writing, and you'll see His presence.

Trust God to guide you to those areas that need your attention. You consciously choose to trust God and rely on Him to lead you. He already knows what He wants you to write and learn. You're just holding the pen.

TOOLS THAT HELP

It is not my intention to present myself as an expert on grief or the academic aspects of grieving. What I am is a survivor of grief work, which has resulted in my discovering strength of character that I never realized I possessed. I offer my experience of grieving and assimilating it into my life. I have allowed it to be absorbed into my heart and spirit and have come through this sacred process whole and much stronger than when I began this journey in May 2000.

I cannot give you a "quick fix" to relieve the pain of grief or expedite the work to be done. No one can do this work for you. There are, however, many who can help, the first of whom is the One who comforts all the afflicted; the One who consoles and heals those who mourn. Ask the Lord to walk with you. He will send His holy helpers to hold your hand, lest you stumble.

THINGS TO REMEMBER

- Use your journal to express those things you cannot talk about. Writing can sometimes be easier than saying it out loud.
- If you are fortunate to have a trusted friend who listens without judgment, talk about what you are feeling.

- Take advantage of bereavement counseling if it is available in your area.
- Be patient; there is no timeline to follow. Your grief is unique and should not be hurried. It is yours. You are the only person to decide when you begin and when you are ready to face your new life.
- Don't be afraid to laugh; it mixes well with tears.
- Get plenty of rest. Learn to relax.
- Eat well. Watch your diet and don't forget your meds.
- There are many good books on grief, so read, read, read.

Widow to Widow, Genevieve Davis Ginsburg
Hope and Help for the Widow, Jan Sheble
Letter to a Grieving Heart, Billy Sprague
Seasons of Grief and Healing, James E Miller
Be Comforted, Gloria Hutchinson
The Free Bird Flies, Bert Fife
Mending the Torn Fabric, Sarah Brabant
Transitions, Julia Cameron

EPILOGUE

Looking Forward

As I healed from my grief, I started to think about my future and what it would look like. I envisioned many things for myself. Travel, writing, beginning a ministry in spiritual direction, being a part of Macy and Sarah lives and especially watching my grandchildren grow up. We have made Bradley's memory an active part of our family life. Macy's son, Bryce feels a connection with his Poppa because of sharing our memories. As of this writing Sarah's daughter, Brooke is three and is just being introduced to Poppa as well.

One of the most wonderful gifts of doing my work of grieving is being open to a new relationship. It was several years after Bradley died that I was able to think and pray about a new beginning with someone. I spoke to God, asking him to help me become healthier, wiser and not be prone to making the old relationship mistakes again. I told Him that if His plan included another partner for me, I wanted to be worthy of this gift.

So I set out doing my work and took the time to take a long, loving look back on my marriage. I asked God to show me the areas where I needed to look in the mirror. I now had the guts and was willing to see my contribution to the marriage that made it vulnerable to outside influences that nearly destroyed it. I never condoned Bradley's infidelities, but I did want to own up to my part of our relationship in every aspect. I certainly didn't want to make the same mistakes again so I asked God to reveal them to me. I realized there were things to change and take with me in my new life as well as things to leave in the past.

I left behind the pain the disappointment when we were not of the same opinion, the same mind or the same heart. I take with me the knowledge that two people are not always on the same wave length. I take with me the belief that I should not expect another person to know my needs or expectations. I must voice them if they stand a chance of being met.

I left behind the need for approval from others. I take with me a new confidence that I am okay just as I am and need no one else's approval.

I left behind all the childish belief that I needed a man to be complete. Even while married, I am still an individual. I had developed a belief that unless I was part of a couple, there was something missing in my life. I take with me a completeness that does not need someone else to make me whole.

I left behind my old-fashioned notions about sexual intimacy. I left behind my inhibitions that stifled and brought boredom to our intimate relationship. I bring with me a willingness to explore my sexuality with no guilt, but only when the time is right.

I left behind the need to rush and keep busy doing, doing, doing, in an effort to avoid my feelings. I take with me a sense of peace and a calm spirit that is quite pleased with doing nothing but being and feeling in the presence of God.

I left behind all the feelings of guilt. I recognize my human weakness and frailty. I did what I could without a script. I take with me the knowledge that this experience has changed me forever. It has remolded my soul and has sobered me in a tremendous way. I accept the fact that I am no longer the same. This new person can have a life without feeling that I don't deserve it.

I journaled many years about the things I left behind and the things I brought with me into this new life. I prayed.

> *My Jesus, I pray, I ask, I plead, help me keep my faith strong and sustaining as I walk this transition from the past to the future. I ask for your will in my life. My will would perhaps not be in my soul's best interest. Show me your path clearly so I cannot mistake it for another that would lead me away from you.*
>
> *I want to honor your love for me always. You know all my desires, my convictions and my failings. I put myself and my future in your hands. You know what is best for me, so I leave all things to you. Help me to take with me only those things that are good for me and leave the rest there they belong in the past. Amen.*

In 2006, God did indeed bless me with meeting a wonderful man, Carl Thanas Broussard. I prayed for a man who was walking with the Lord and would be able to honor Bradley's memory. Carl is indeed a very devout Catholic with a strong devotion to family. He says he even prays for intercession to Bradley about how to love me the way God loves me. I could not have asked for a better companion to spend this second half of life with. His generosity as I have worked on this book about my life before him is remarkable. I never dreamed God would bless me with love a second time. I think I was always meant to be married to a Broussard.

An Apple of My Dreams

An apple a day, that's what they say.
If I reach for the apple of my dreams, I'm afraid people will see the bite I take.
They might say, "Hey, don't take too big of a bite, stay where it's safe."
Whose voice keeps me from taking my apple out of the shadows? As I decipher the tones and words, I realize it's my own voice, coming from a place that doesn't have the brave soil for cultivation of apples.
A timid little voice heard from the center of a garden with space for the smallest Fuji apple.

This safe little apple is tasted on rare occasions.
A small bite bravely swallowed, leaving all that remains for applesauce.
The flesh is pulverized till there is no zest left to surprise the palate. It can even be eaten with no teeth.

An apple a day, that's what they say.
If I am to taste the apple of my dreams, I must first decide what kind of apple I like.
Is it the Red Delicious, Granny Smith or Gala?
I overturn all the soil in my garden to discover the big, bright, Red Delicious apple, with its shiny outer skin that is solid and juicy to the core.

No safe little Fuji apple for this new apple taster, and by all means, no applesauce either.
I am weary of choosing to have a small bite and even the apple-sauce for the sake of keeping the old garden safe.

It's my apple and I choose to taste it with the biggest bite I can take. I will savor every bite of my apple, seeds and all!

*And guess what, all you applesauce eaters?
I might even eat the stem!
And when I'm done with that, I will plant an apple tree in the garden of my soul, where dreams flourish and only brave apples grow.*

*An apple a day, that's what they say.
I say "Bon Appétit!"*

It is my prayer that in sharing my journey through grief, you have been strengthened to journey on with hope. It is important to remember our experiences and what they have taught us. If we don't remember their lessons, they become worthless and of little value. We all know the sacred memories of our loved ones will never be forgotten. However, the lessons of grieving should be shared forward so others who travel down this road will be encouraged to find their courage, their guts to "do the work" of grief and find their life anew.

If we have the guts to "do" the work of grieving, remembering our experiences and the lessons they teach us, we will be able to let God heal our broken hearts and receive the grace He has for us. What you keep bottled up has the potential to destroy if it festers inside. What you allow to come forth can bring with it healing and new life.

God does have the grace; please find the guts. You won't ever regret it. The choice is yours to make. God bless you.

My Magnificat

My soul dances with joy at the sound of the Father
calling my name.
I go to Him, unafraid and trusting, and rest myself.
I am home at last.
Thank you my Jesus, my Christ, for making the way
that I might delight in my Father's company.

You, O Lord, are my salvation, my refuge, my sanctuary.
No enemy can reach me as long as I remain with you.
It is in you alone, my Heavenly Father, that I place my trust and
my hope.

It is you I love.
You satisfy every desire of my heart.

I want to worship you all the days of my life.
Let me never be put to shame because my sin has
come between us.

Show me your ways Father.
Show me your heart.
Let all that I am love you more each day.

I desire Your will for me Father, Your will.
All this I pray through your Son, Jesus Christ,
my Lord and my Savior.
Amen.

Appendix A

POETRY BY JOAN THERIOT-BROUSSARD

BE STILL AND KNOW

Lord, this is what you ask of me and you mean it in many areas.
We must allow you to be God.
We must step quietly to the side of life's parade of people, duties, and pace of this world.
We must step to the quiet and be still, as a soft breeze rustles the leaves.

We must step to the sound of the quiet and listen to the rummages of God as he plies, pulls and works this little piece of clay in his gentle mighty hands.
We must step to the quiet peace and allow him to be God; and in that quiet we can receive the gift of surrender, of acceptance, of total dependence on God.

The steps to the quiet are not taken without much stumbling and back tracking.
At first it may seem you have taken a step to the quiet, only to realize it was just a tip-toe to another place in the world, and still you are dependant on people, on places, on things.
These are not what the place of quiet stillness is made of.

The place of quiet stillness is a safe haven for the sad and the grieving.
The place of quiet stillness is a warm caring embrace for the lonely, for the one left behind.
The place of quiet stillness is a place of wisdom, for if you choose to go there, you will learn that all things of this world are to pass way and only God's love will remain.
You will learn that people can only do so much with their limited capacity to love and understand.

You will learn that no one can bring you to the place of quiet stillness.
You must take these steps alone, with your faith guiding you and God leading the way.
You will learn the way to know that He is God.
No human being can make you see this.
Only God and teach God.
And for Him to teach and you to finally learn,
you must be still and know that he is God.

SHAVED HEADS
In they come, one after the other, a son, a brother and a best friend.
All with smooth heads that match the one lying in the bed.
A gesture of love shown to one unaware.
They join him on the journey through pain and suffering.
With shaved heads, they join hands, hearts and march on.
A son speaks his intention "As long as you have no hair, neither will I."
The brothers alike, not much to shave, but much love to offer.

It's been many years since that journey has ended.
and only some of the hair has grown back.
The memory of those shaved heads gives witness to a gesture offered in love
to one not thinking he deserved it.
That one now has hair only heaven can see.
I'm sure he looks down on those heads and thinks.
"What love they showed to me."

NORMAL IS DIFFERENT NOW

This all feels too "big" to pray about;
so many feelings, so much emotion, so intense.
I don't have words to describe everything I feel.
It is very time consuming, this caregiver role.
There just is not much time without something to do.
Lord Jesus, help me to be faithful.
You have humbled me with many blessings; even in the midst of this illness.
All I want is to serve you.
I do so, as I care for your servant, my husband.
I realize that our lives will never be the same; never to return as it was before.
Normal will be different now.
It is hard to handle not knowing where this will all lead.
How will he be?
How bad will it get?
How will it end?
Will he suffer?
I have so many questions.
I am anxious about the future.
I know I should take one day at a time. This I will strive to do.

A MEMORY GIFT

A memory can have a life of its own.
A moment can be so tender and delicate and yet so vivid and strong.
It is not diminished by time or distance.
It becomes a memory gift.
This memory gift presents its feeling, circumstance and detail to sustain us in times of sadness.
It was a brief moment and yet it had the depth of a lifetime.
It was two hearts reaching and touching, telling of love without speaking.
Many things can be said without words and be understood between those who love.
This exchange; simple, renewing and nourishes in times of loneliness.
It was a day when reality was harsh and cruel but held a gift and could last a lifetime.
Sitting, his legs weakening as the illness robbed his strength and our future.
We hugged, we kissed.
We held each other wishing this could go on forever.
While being held in the arms of my love, I pray...

"God, please put this moment in my memory in the category of ones to last forever, never to be forgotten, or diminished even slightly by the passing of time. It must be my hug to remember when he is no longer here to hold me."

BELOVED

A thin veil of lies that lay neatly over my eyes, preventing the view of the truth;
misguiding, causing doubt of my place in this world.
A thin veil of lies that lay neatly over my heart preventing the revelation of truth about love and its source.
A thin veil of lies lay neatly over my ears blocking the sound of thee Father calling the real me forth.
A thin veil of lies lay neatly over my mouth stifling authentic praise, real growth and genuine living.

A thin veil of lies lifted by one simple word, "Beloved".
One word and the life you long for springs up like the red spider lily that suddenly appears;
it has grown and matured underground, unseen, bringing forth precious blossoms.

You will feel my love fill you from a source within.
You have remained faithful to this source of all love
in spite of the thin veil of lies that life has laid neatly over your soul.

My Beloved, let there be no more veils, no more lies.
Live in love.
Live in truth.
Live in faith that I am with you always.

HOPE, ONE TO ANOTHER

When you are sad or lonely, I will throw you a rope.
When you are falling in the "hole" of despair,
you can count on my toss to reach you with hope.

A rope of love and empathy
A rope of heartstrings, woven together to form a braid
strong enough to rescue both the caller and the rescuer.

Both will be rescued, one from brokenness and
another from shared pain.
Both will reach the heights of healing and joy together.

Their shared experience binds them as though tied together
at the heart by a divine strand that begins and ends with the
divine rope maker.

A knot of hope on each end - because as I toss the rope to rescue you,
I am rescued on the other end.
The rescuer becomes the rescued and the sacred cycle continues

We shall walk this road together
with courage and faith, hand-in-hand with God;
Jesus has paved the way of this road with his sacrifice.
Let us walk on toward our future
with newfound courage to face whatever lies ahead.

A FAITHFUL SERVANT

As I walk out into the morning I am filled with life refreshed.
The air is cool and crisp.
I can hear the leaves rustling in the trees as the wind moves them.
The birds are happy too; I hear them sing to each other.
The precious hummers are here too.

This change in the weather is a welcomed one.
It has been hot and dry.
Brown patches of dead grass spot the lawn.

This weather makes me glad to be alive.
Thank you Lord for this gift of my life.
You are such a wonderful and generous creator.

The sun, a faithful servant of yours, is coming up to dry the dew and light the day.
If only it were as easy as the sun coming up each day
to warm the hearts of those who stay away from you.

I pray that this sun, this day will radiate your warmth into the coldest
of hearts and its rays of light carry your love into the deepest corners of those souls.

HUMANS AND HUMMERS

Coffee is good. Air is cool.
The patio is comfortable and my rocker is quiet, no squeaks.

The birds wake the day with their melodies.
Perhaps they are telling each other of their plans for the day.

And the hummers; tiny but so energetic. Always on the go.
They are incapable of slowing down, lest they die.
This is the pace meant for them.
It is as natural as the sun.

They remind me of myself.
Never being still and always ready to fly off to the next feeder.
For humans, this pace is not the norm.
We are meant to travel slower so we can enjoy God's creations.
We are not meant to dash here and there worrying about our territory and keeping it all for ourselves.

God meant for us to depend on him for our needs and to share what we have.
These little hummers, the tiniest of birds have much to teach about how to live,
Or should I say, how not to live.

Appendix B

PONDER AND REFLECT

Reflecting on Your Journey through Grief

The following reflection questions can be very beneficial in doing your grief "work". I trust you will find the guts to begin just as I am trusting God to give you the grace to persevere and heal your heart, renew your spirit and return you to a life of joy and happiness.

Use these reflection questions as your need requires. It is good to journal your responses to each prompt or question. Do them slowly and don't rush to finish. You many spend several days thinking and journaling on one, while moving quicker through others. The goal is to allow your spirit to move you through healing.

These reflections can be covered alone, with a trusted companion or with a group in a safe environment.

- What event in my history has impacted my life the most? What has helped me cope in the past?
  Prayer suggestions:
  >Psalm 40: 1-6: Prayer for help
  >Psalm 139: 1-18: God's infinite care

- Re-read the poem, "What Our Eyes have seen". Ponder, reflect and journal your feelings.

- What do sadness, anger, fear and grief mean to you? How would you describe your grief as progressing, and/or digressing?

- The task of grief is looking at our loss and come to terms with the new reality of what this loss means to you. This is the hard work we must do and usually what we resist the most. Describe the roles your loved one played in your life.

- What is most longed for in those roles? What is easier to let go of?

- Ponder and reflect about a memory of your loved one that often comes to mind.

- Think about the high points in your life with your loved one: celebrations, births, vacations or special times spent together. Journal your feelings.

- Think about the low points in your life with your loved one: hard times, worries, tragedies, betrayals and misunderstandings. Journal your feelings.

- Re-read the poem, "Forgive Me". Ponder, reflect and journal your feelings.

- What unfinished business with your loved one do you carry?

- Are there any issues you feel you need to apologize for?

- Are there issues for which you would like to forgive your loved one?

- What does "letting go" mean to you?

- Unfinished Business/Sense of Incompleteness:
    1. What has been left undone?
    2. What words have been left unsaid?
    3. What would it take to come to terms with the uncompleted aspects of your relationship?
    4. Saying Goodbye: Write a letter to your loved one?

- What other factors, unrelated to your grief, are contributing to stress right now?

- Describe what life is like without your loved one.

- Are you allowing yourself to grieve? Describe how, or why not? What works for you? What do you need?
- Write a letter **to you** from your loved one. Let your true, authentic self, the one that holds wisdom, sit with you as you write this special letter. (Take dictation from them.)
- Re-read poem, "An Apple of My Dreams". Ponder, reflect and journal your feelings about how you will journey on?

About the Author

Joan Theriot-Broussard currently lives in Youngsville, Louisiana. She completed her studies in Spiritual Direction at the St. Charles Retreat Center, in the Diocese of Lake Charles, Louisiana, under the directorship of Father Don Piraro. She has been providing Spiritual Direction since 2007. She is a member of Spiritual Directors International and serves on the Board of Directors for Louisiana Spiritual Directors.

She been giving retreats on Spiritual Journaling since 2004 and has been journaling her own prayer for over 30 years. Joan also gives other retreats, such as Journaling through Grief, which includes a six-week follow-up series on journaling our grief.

Joan serves her parish as Lector, Eucharistic Minister, and serves on the Parish Council for St. Anne Roman Catholic Church in Youngsville, where she lives with her husband, Carl.

She is a published author and has written several magazine articles on the gifts of the sacraments. Joan is a Hospice of Acadiana volunteer.

Join the conversations on her blog,
http://standingfaithful.wordpress.com

I would love to hear how you found the guts to work through your grief, allowed God's grace to heal your wounds and your experience of journaling it all.

107 Beacon Drive,
Youngsville, LA 70592

www.ingramcontent.com/pod-product-compliance
Lightning Source LLC
Chambersburg PA
CBHW021410290426
44108CB00010B/467